Marketing Iceberg

FARHAD MK

Copyright © 2020 Farhad MK

All rights reserved.

ISBN: 9798580070438

Table of Contents

Introduction: Page 5

Chapter 1: Understanding the Unconscious: Page 8

   Unconscious development: Page 8

   Unconscious expansion: Page 12

   Unconscious in the 21st Century: Page 15

Chapter 2: The Psychographic Pathway: Page 23

Chapter 3: Artificial Intelligence in Marketing: Page 29

Chapter 4: Advanced Analytics and the New Age of Marketing: Page 34

   Psychology-driven Algorithms: Page 37

Chapter 5: Giving New Meaning to Old Traditions: Page 43

   Context is King: Page 46

   Analytic Creativity: Page 49

Chapter 6: Ethics and Privacy in the Age of Big Data: Page 52

   Creative Destruction: Page 56

Conclusion: Page 59

MARKETING ICEBERG

Introduction

This handbook explores how data scientists, using data mining and data harvesting to penetrate our minds, and in the process gain deep insights into our psychological behaviour. These data scientists use our mind's conscious and unconscious domains to influence our thought processes, compelling us to make decisions without even knowing it. This approach is far from simple, which explains why so few companies invest the time and money in understanding it. Usually, this approach requires highly specialized and experienced data experts — including web analysts, algorithm specialists, data engineers, and the like — who possess a strong working knowledge of the human brain. These data experts combine this strong working knowledge with artificial intelligence, such as predictive analytics and machine learning, to create desired responses from people like you and I. This works on a micro scale, like Amazon recommending a new spatula based on the pot we already purchased, or on a macro scale, like Cambridge Analytica influencing election outcomes across the globe. This handbook is meant to provide insights into the human psyche, and explain how firms that are intently focused on our decisions can influence us in profound ways.

Our discussion will start with the mind, specifically its unconscious domains which have long perplexed researchers. This handbook will delve into how our understanding of the unconscious has morphed and expanded, from Sigmund Freud's 20th Century work in psychoanalysis, to its integration with business and marketing at the turn of the century. We will then shift our focus to psychographic segmentation, and examine how this type of targeting enables firms to better understand the unconscious, and its impacts on our lifestyle and behaviour. After a brief overview of artificial intelligence, we will segue to a larger discussion about business analytics or advanced analytics, which has created untold opportunities in many industries, including marketing. This focus on data mining provides marketers with deep insights about our thoughts, enabling them to influence our behaviour in profound ways. We will then look into the value of traditional marketing activities and how the data mining activities become valuable inputs into the creation of truly impactful identities and messaging. We will conclude our discussion by highlighting some of big data's ethical and privacy implications.

This handbook is intended for new and existing entrepreneurs, startup founders, marketing enthusiasts and students, business owners, consultants, and political strategists. This handbook does not have a political undercurrent. That is not to say, however, that this dimension is unimportant. Strong moral foundations are essential in our daily lives, and all businesses should prioritize the ongoing implementation of a robust business ethics framework that guides their decision-making. This handbook is meant to provide its readers with insightful information about human psychology and marketing-specific data science that is properly contextualized using real world research and company case studies. It does not act as, and should not be construed as, a political or public relations effort to pass judgement on the actions of any organization based on ideological leanings. Rather, this handbook provides readers with information about our brains, decision-making process, valuable marketing tools, and pertinent company examples, all of which should better position the reader for success in this digitized, data-driven world.

MARKETING ICEBERG

Chapter 1: Understanding the Unconscious

Unconscious development

The unconscious mind has long perplexed researchers. Even dating back as recently as the early-20th Century, the unconscious mind was a great source of frustration for prevailing academic psychologists. At the time, behaviorism was beginning to grow its roots in the academic community. Advocates for the behaviorism theory, or behaviorists as they became known, believed that human and other animal behaviors were learned from two sources: reflexes and lived history. In the case of the former, reflexive behaviour was learned as a result of our response to stimuli, like events or environments. Subjects would respond to stimuli in a way that maximized positive consequences and minimized negative consequences. Put differently, an event or situation occurs, which then leads to a response from the subject who wants to maximize positive outcomes and minimize negative ones. The other source of behavior, history, would over time have an impact as well, since the subject would experience the consequences of an action, and respond accordingly the next time.[1] For instance, an event occurs, the child subject responds with rage, and then the parent punishes the child; this lived experience, along with other similar ones, forces the child subject to understand that a rage-filled response will only lead to negative consequences, and hence the subject in the future will attempt to minimize that by modifying their behavior.

This behaviorism theory began to grow in prominence around the same time that another theory of the mind started to gain traction in the mainstream. Sigmund Freud's foundational work in psychoanalysis focused on the unconscious mind, namely the theories and therapies used to study and uncover its depth. In Freud's view, these theories and therapies could be used to better understand the human psyche and even treat mental illnesses. Freud likened the human mind to an iceberg which had three levels: the tip, the middle, and the submerged portions.[2] The tip represents the conscious mind, which includes all of the accessible mental processes, like our thoughts and feelings. Provided we can think and talk about them in way that is rational, they are considered part of the conscious mind.[3] As an example, consider the clothes you are wearing. You can probably describe your shirt and pants, explain why you chose to wear them instead of your other clothes today, and why you might consider wearing the same outfit again sometime in the future. The iceberg's middle level consists of our preconscious, which are thoughts that may not be present in our mind but we can recall easily into our consciousness for use.[4] Consider your phone number, for example. You likely were not thinking about it before I mentioned the words phone number, but you can now raise it up to your conscious level and recall it with ease. That is your preconscious. Finally, we have the underwater portion of the iceberg which, as we know from the Titanic, matters a great deal and has a huge impact on the future. This submerged portion of our mind, called the unconscious, is far greater in size than both the tip (conscious) and the middle (preconscious). The unconscious state can be considered a repository that has stored inside of it all of our repressed memories, feelings, thoughts, and the like.[5] Information that is unpleasant, bothersome, traumatic, or anxiety-inducing — say witnessing abuse as a child — would fall under this unconscious category.

It is not surprising that behaviorists, and other

more empirical researchers, took issue with Freud's theories. Behaviorists, certainly during the first half of the 20th Century, believed that researchers should use objective descriptions and tests as the basis for theorizing. From a behaviorist standpoint, Freud's focus on the unconscious made any meaningful objective description and testing difficult — if not impossible.[6] There was no way, at least based on the scientific and psychological approaches at the time, to prove or disprove Freud's theory. As a result, the unconscious specifically and psychoanalysis broadly were not considered legitimate according to the scientific community at the time. As science and psychology continued to advance, though, it became apparent that the unconscious, in its vast size and influence, could no longer be ignored.

Unconscious expansion

While Freud's theory of the unconscious may have lacked the same sort of scientific rigor as traditional psychological and scientific disciplines, his contribution was still significant. Freud was not the first to discern differences between our conscious state and our unconscious state, but he was instrumental in popularizing the distinction in the mainstream, which meant that the unconscious began to get the attention it rightfully deserved. It was not long after Freud's views were published that cognitive and social psychologists began to research and confirm key ideas concerning the unconscious, including identifying unconscious processes like procedural memory,[7] automatic processing such as muscle memory[8] and implicit bias,[9] wherein humans have attitudes and stereotypes about others without consciously knowing it. Even if we accurately concede that Freud was off the mark in regards to the unconscious, then he was off the mark for reasons that do not align with his behaviorist critics. That is, Freud in many respects underestimated the scope and influence of the unconscious, which covers far more mental processes than Freud originally theorized.[10] It is easier, for instance, to view the unconscious as a lone, singular, solitary entity; however, it has become apparent, through our understanding of universal grammar and even facial recognition, that our unconscious has countless different domains or modules operating at once, each responsible for managing its own affairs.[11][12] Furthermore, the unconscious does not necessarily repress certain thoughts because they are uncomfortable; instead the unconscious is actually able to adapt and process most of our mind's information far more efficiently than our conscious state,[13] which helps explain why so much of what humans do remains, as Freud would say, underwater.

Unconscious in the 21st Century

It would be an understatement to suggest that a lot has changed since Freud's 20th Century theorizing. The way we move, communicate, and act have all changed fundamentally, thanks in large part to new technologies that have re-shaped our world. Our perspective of the unconscious, too, has changed and morphed over time. The unconscious went from being material that was great for cocktail parties, to becoming the guiding subject matter of academic research and studies. Dr. Gerald Zaltman, Harvard Business School Professor, knows this all too well, as the turn of the 21st Century brought with it new opportunities to understand human impulses.

Over the better part of the last two decades, Dr. Zaltman has not been shy about his acceptance of the unconscious, nor has he been shy about it being the overwhelming force influencing human decision-making.[14] Zaltman has questioned the presumption that people actually know what they think. In doing so, Zaltman and other researchers have been instrumental in marketing's monumental change.

Zaltman and Freud to the very least have shared a belief that humans are not necessarily truthful or forthright about certain thoughts and feelings, because these thoughts and feelings are driven by unconscious urges, like emotions, of which humans are unaware. Such urges are buried in the unconscious, and otherwise inaccessible to us. When called upon, we may respond with our beliefs, explanations and justifications, but these are just surface-level judgements; our true motivations lie somewhere beneath. It is difficult for us to say truthfully what we think when we do not know what we feel. Zaltman's main priority was to overcome this hurdle, and to uncover ways to understand human emotions more reliably.

As a quick exercise, take a second to think about

an advertising campaign that moved you. No, not one that moved you to click "SKIP AD" on Youtube after 5 seconds, but one that, upon reflection, you can recall easily and you feel was a great advertisement. Was it inspiring or sentimental? Did you feel warm inside, perhaps a strong connection to your loved ones? Did it make you hungry, adventurous, or aroused? Was it humorous? How excited were you to see the ad again? All of these questions matter, because they indicate how important emotions are when formulating an opinion. Notice in that line of questioning how little is focused on the product or service, its features, or where the company originates. Well-made products with superior functionality can fail horribly in the market, not because of poor quality, but because their marketing simply does not resonate with the emotions of the target market.

It was on this basis that Zaltman declared that "95% of all cognition, all the thinking that drives our decisions and behaviors, occurs unconsciously — and that includes consumer decisions".[15] Marketers had been placing too much stock in the 5 percent that was conscious, and had become misguided in their use of traditional methods to penetrate the 95% that was unseen. As it became clear, these traditional methods of understanding consumer sensibilities had been wholly ineffective, forcing Zaltman and others to think outside of the box.

Dr. Zaltman, for his part, developed in response the Zaltman Metaphor Elicitation Technique (ZMET). This approach employs pictures as a way to uncover the feelings of human subjects. Participants are asked to bring in pictures that encapsulate their feelings about using a name brand product and its generic alternative. After a comprehensive two-hour interview with the subject, the interviewer would assemble the images together and create a collage of all of the images. Even though each participant brought in different pictures, and each collage was visually distinct, all participants had exhibited the identical inner feelings about why they use the name brand instead of the generic brand.[16]

This creative approach represented a departure from the standard marketing approach, which was heavy on focus groups and surveys. Interestingly, Zaltman's training as a mathematical sociologist gave him insights on the types of sentiments surveys were good at capturing, and the ones they were not good at capturing. The key for Zaltman and other marketers was to devise exciting new methods to reveal the consumers' hidden motivations in a way that was not infused with the surveyors' own bias, and did not give us insights that departed diametrically from the truth.[17]

As mentioned previously, Zaltman seemed to confirm something that was suspected but could not be verified: that people do not always tell the truth about their thoughts and urges. You can see how this would severely complicate surveyors' job, since truthful responses represent the bedrock of their work. That said, people may not reveal the truth unintentionally or intentionally. For instance, it could be done unintentionally due to people not knowing what they feel deep down, or because people struggle to properly explain their feelings. This could also be done intentionally due to people fearing what others might think of their true feelings, which causes them to hide their actual views from surveyors. This dynamic will be addressed later in more detail, particularly as it relates to political opinions, however it is worth noting that this is a dynamic that can skew perspectives. Regardless of whether it is unintentional or intentional, it seems clear that people are thinking and acting based on their unconscious; however, how does the conscious factor into this? Interestingly, the conscious goes to work almost immediately after the initial emotions have been registered in our body, by coming up with rational or logical explanations about those emotions. This can help justify the feelings in our minds, or even help us finally act on the impulses. In either scenario, the conscious mind is active and working at the direction of the unconscious, rationalizing emotions up to, and even after, the point of action.

Zaltman was clear in noting that different tools should be used for different purposes.[18] There is a saying in boxing that "styles make fights," which means each boxer has their own way of fighting, and certain boxers, because of their training and approach, may be better suited to confront a particular challenger, which makes for an interesting fight. In marketing, tools like surveys and focus groups may be useful depending on your predicament, your industry, your sector, and your ideal outcome; however, these tools are valuable only if they are catered to your situation, and you should consider all variables — including the drawbacks — prior to relying on these tools, and the data you get from them. When you are mindful and considerate of these dynamics, you can create interesting outcomes for your venture.

Zaltman understood that people think based on metaphors and symbols, which create powerful associations and influence behaviour. The challenge for marketers was about taking these powerful symbols, and understanding them as a collection of actions. It was about starting at the end — with associations and ideal images — and working backwards. By understanding individual characteristics and lifestyles, perhaps marketers could gain more insights into the specific unconscious actions that create and sustain symbolic associations.

Chapter 2: The Psychographic Pathway

As we strive to understand how marketers use our unconscious feelings for profit, particularly in an age characterized by artificial intelligence, we should first spend some time focusing on how marketers approach the complex task of data mining, because data mining is an essential input in creating artificial intelligence that is responsive and relevant. Consider this: when starting a project, you usually get going by researching the project's subject matter. You can start researching the topic generally, but you will soon find that in order to gain a deeper understanding, you will have to be more specific in your research. Details matter, and by doing deeper and more specific research, you will be able to better understand your project's intricacies, which will help in project planning and execution further down the line.

Marketing is no different. When starting a venture, you consider your product or service, and you research the industry and possible competitors. As these details become clear, your lens becomes more focused, allowing you to really delve into the specifics of your market. There are several different routes you can take to break down, or segment, your market, with each route offering its own approaches to reaching the target market. In other words, HOW you segment your market matters. There is demographic segmentation which focuses on age, gender, income, education and other such characteristics, behavioral segmentation which focuses on the spending and purchasing habits of people in your market, and geographic segmentation that focuses on regional considerations like city and climate that could impact those in your market. The final, psychographic segmentation, is one such approach that has grown increasingly important in our diverse, multi-faceted world, offering gateways to better understand the impulses driving human decision-making.

Psychographic segmentation involves categorizing or grouping potential consumers based on their personalities and individual characteristics. Psychographic segmentation, as the name alludes, refers to psychological traits — like personality attributes, values and attitudes, lifestyles choices, motivations, and priorities — that influence people's buying habits.[19] Whereas the demographic, behavioral, and geographic segmentations tend to be fairly straightforward, psychographic segmentation is much more time-consuming and challenging to pin down. Psychographic segmentation does not start with data points, nor does it involve surface-level information, like age, user status, or city. Psychographic segmentation is not immediately data-centric because it is highly subjective, and hence it requires painstaking research and data collection in order to uncover the details.[20] Despite the time and effort involved, there is considerable upside to the psychographic segmentation approach, namely that it allows marketers to understand their market's intricacies by cutting across demographic and geographic differences, and arriving at a more contextualized market segment. Just as the mindset of customers plays into the design and development of a product or service, the mindset of customers plays into how experts market a product. In this way, we should consider psychographics as a way to both categorize the market, as well as connect to the market. Let us briefly consider an example.

As we know, Apple Inc. today presides over one of the most valuable brands in the world, and is known for producing a variety of gadgets for personal and professional purposes. This was not always the case. After more than a decade away from Apple, Steve Jobs in 1996 inherited a company that was struggling for market share and seemingly had minimal prospects for a positive future. In order to remind customers of Apple's longstanding commitment to innovation, the company together with its advertising partner created the "Think Different" campaign. The simple campaign would show images of visionaries throughout the ages — including Gandhi, Einstein, and Jim Henson — and include the tagline "Think Different". By merely associating its brand with important thinkers throughout history, Apple was insinuating that the foremost thinkers of our time would be using Apple products if they were alive. Target consumers did not want to be just another person, or think the same way that everyone else thinks; rather, the target consumers — no matter their age, gender, city of residence, or purchasing habits — wanted to embrace a challenging lifestyle, aspire to something greater, and create a positive impact on the world. Needless to say the campaign was a success, and Apple has used a similar philosophy in marketing its products since. The company heavily focuses on psychographic traits that can appeal to men and women, teenagers and adults, Americans and non-Americans, and various other market segments. From the first iPod to the latest iPhone, Apple has been committed to psychographic segmentation, focusing on such attributes as lifestyle, passions, hopes, and interests as a means to market and appeal to target consumers.

As we can see, psychographic segmentation remains a powerful, if not difficult, way to segment and target consumers. It is a detailed method used by companies and marketers and, when effective, psychographic segmentation can lead to the development of products, services and messaging that appeal more directly to the unconscious impulses of target consumers. Soon, you will see how psychographic segmentation factors into artificial intelligence and how, in this new age of marketing, we can gain valuable insights into consumers' unconscious.

MARKETING ICEBERG

Chapter 3: Artificial Intelligence in Marketing

When we think about artificial intelligence as a concept, our minds naturally gravitate towards science fiction universes. The Phillip K. Dick novels of yesterday and the big budget Hollywood films of today have given us wild impressions about what artificial intelligence means for the future of the 21st Century. The likes of Stephen Hawking and Elon Musk have not been shy expressing their fear that robots, equipped with artificial intelligence, will reach singularity. This, of course, is a fancy way of saying robots will eventually become self-aware and come after us like Terminator — yikes! As interesting as that topic is, it is probably best reserved for creative writers, movie producers, neuroscientists, engineers, and philosophy aficionados. For the rest of us, even on the most basic of levels, artificial intelligence strives to make simple the tasks that are complicated and tedious. In the span of a single day, we use artificial intelligence to unlock our phones (facial recognition), navigate our way to and from a destination (map software), decide on a purchase (Amazon search and recommendation algorithm), and even converse online with a company representative (receiving tech support online from a chatbot).

Depending on your source of information, there are many different ways to classify artificial intelligence and its related parts. Our environments have become oriented to the digital, and with every advancement comes an opportunity to further integrate artificial intelligence, which creates a new standard of what is — and is not — artificial intelligence. For the sake of simplicity, artificial intelligence can be broadly understood as machines that think like humans. These machines can mimic certain human thought processes and actions, including predicting outcomes of future events and even potentially learning new things. We will focus on both of these possibilities and their relevance to marketing in subsequent sections.

Let us first ensure, before delving into advanced analytics and machine learning, that we have operational definitions for some key terms we will be using throughout the remainder of this piece. Big data refers to the analysis of large amounts of data through non-traditional software. More specifically, big data can also refer to the methods used to extract value from data. Data can be structured or unstructured, which means that data can be organized and searchable, or data can be raw and free of a defined format. Approximately 20% of the world's data is structured while 80% of data is unstructured.[21] Data in itself is not useful or useless; data is simply there, and once that data is structured and injected with meaning by data scientists, it becomes relevant to understanding human behavior.

Interestingly, cloud computing has created new opportunities for us in relation to big data. Today, data analysts can acquire data and automatically store it through cloud computing software. These clouds, and the information they contain, can be accessed from anywhere. This mode of collection more easily allows data analysts to engage in data mining. Data mining, a popular term in our digital world, refers to the practice of finding patterns in data. These data patterns are then used to identify interesting consumer and markets trends, which are subsequently used by businesses for targeting activities.

Businesses that effectively use data and augmented intelligence can create competitive advantages and even re-engineer our way of thinking. In these cases, artificial intelligence can influence our unconscious mind to make decisions before we even know it. No matter the objective, opportunities in the artificial intelligence space are plentiful. These opportunities arise when firms are able to capture large amounts of data, engage in data mining, and ultimately operationalize that data in ways where it targets specific emotions, eliciting the desired response from the target market.

The following section will focus on advanced analytics or business analytics. Advanced analytics is a form of big data that, ideally, allows us to more reliably predict future outcomes before they happen. It has broad-based application, and can be used by businesses, political strategists, and especially fantasy sports enthusiasts. When combined with psychographic segmentation and data mining, predictive analytics can be a powerful tool in gaging future human sentiments and capitalizing off of trends. Machine learning, for its part, can also be combined with big data, which in essence allows machines to adapt and learn constantly based on newly added information. We will soon understand how businesses are able to leverage such analytical tools to gain entry into our unconscious minds.

Chapter 4: Advanced Analytics and the New Age of Marketing

The marketing world since the turn of the century has not been alone in embracing the power of advanced analytics. In fact, we can credit America's favourite pastime for popularizing advanced analytics, and especially its close cousin — predictive analytics. Moneyball, a book written by Michael Lewis in 2003 and subsequently turned into a movie by the same name in 2011, was more than just a story about baseball statistics or "sabermetrics"; what started as an experiment to marginally improve win totals for a moribund baseball franchise turned into a case study on advanced analytics' effectiveness in a real world environment. It was a watershed moment because it signalled a mindset shift that moved an entire industry from its traditional confines and into the modern era. Today, advanced analytics has become a guiding force in assessing roster production, projected wins, player effectiveness in offensive and defensive positions, and much more across ALL major sports. More than anything, it helped us understand that data and details matter when crafting a winning strategy.

How do predictive analytics factor into marketing? Specifically, how have big data and data mining helped advanced analytics become a guiding force in marketing? In order to understand this, let us first examine advanced analytics, or business analytics, more closely.

Advanced analytics generally refers to a form of data analysis that uses sophisticated tools and methods to uncover insights and develop recommendations. These analytical tools and methods are considered advanced because they are able to conduct the complex types of analyses that traditional business intelligence cannot. Advanced analytics, or as it is sometimes referred to as business analytics, consists of three main subsets: descriptive analytics, predictive analytics, and prescriptive analytics.

Descriptive analytics is the most common of the three, and involves mining historical data to understand the reasons for past performances. Both successes and failures are analyzed using business data as inputs, including sales, marketing, financial and operational data. In essence, descriptive analytics gives firms a good idea of "what happened" and may even let firms know "why it happened". Predictive analytics, like the name suggests, is focused on predicting likely future outcomes before they happen. Predictive analytics gives meaning to historical data by using algorithms, rules and possibly external data to identify trends and the probability of future outcomes coming to fruition. Predictive analytics is really about "what is likely to happen". Not to be outdone, prescriptive analytics is the third variety of advanced analytics. It does the job of predictive analytics, but also delves deeper into why certain events occurred; in doing so, prescriptive analytics provides myriad options about what to do and what not to do, as well as each option's implications. Further, prescriptive analytics can take in large amounts of new data — structured data and unstructured data — and provide constantly updating analytical information, which improves the accuracy of predictions as well as options. Prescriptive analytics, then, is not just about "what is likely to happen," but also about "what happens after that" and "what can we do to take advantage of what will happen". In this way, advanced analytics — through descriptive analytics, predictive analytics, and prescriptive analytics — can provide insights into the past, present and future, thereby improving a firm's likelihood of success.

Now that we know what advanced analytics entails, let us examine what it means to firms. In order to do this, let us consider a modern, yet notorious example from the political world: Cambridge Analytica. But first, some context.

Psychology-driven Algorithms

Michal Kosinski is a Stanford University professor who holds a doctorate in psychology. Dr. Kosinski's work focuses on computational psychology, and examines personal differences in behavior, desires, and performance. Dr. Kosinski believes algorithms are full of potential, enabling pattern recognition and improving our predictive power. More specifically, algorithms are great at predicting human traits, like predicting specific emotions with a high degree of accuracy.[22] How? Well, every time we do anything digitally, especially over the internet, we leave behind our digital footprints, which Kosinski contests amounts to 2 gigabytes per person, per day![23] Firms engage in data mining to extract secondary data from this initial source. This can include more than just simple geographic location; in fact, if phone and software manufacturers know where you are, they can aggregate that data and extract even more information, including your lifestyle, religious and political views, health status, age, gender, and more.[24] As discussed previously, these psycho-demographic traits are valuable since they can provide insights into the otherwise hidden dimensions of the unconscious. Equipped with this information, firms can target us with increasingly specific messaging that appeals directly to our urges, interests, values and preferences, all of which they know thanks to big data.

We can see this in action every time we log into Youtube, Amazon, Spotify or Facebook. How many times have you clicked on one of Youtube's recommended videos? Have you ever purchased through Amazon an item that was suggested to you while browsing? Perhaps you recently downloaded a new song from an artist based on a recommendation you received from Spotify, or you decided to tap "add friend" when you saw an acquaintance under the "Suggested Friends" category. All of these recommendations and suggestions are based on your digital footprint and are generated through data mining. Data analysts then use this data in algorithms that ensure any and all recommendations are in tune with your preferences.[25] Much like data, algorithms are not good or bad; algorithms are simply there, created by humans to perform specific actions. The most worrisome element, then, is not the algorithms themselves, but the all too human element which can entice individuals to use algorithms for nefarious purposes.

Cambridge Analytica, under the purview of psychographic segmentation, engaged in "behavioral microtargeting," a term that refers to direct marketing which is targeted and predictive. This approach when applied to politics allows firms to understand which issues really impact an important subset of voters, how a person really feels about a party or candidate, and how a person's needs shift over time. Needless to say this information is incredibly valuable to political parties who have abundant yet finite resources, and need to strategically allocate these resources to optimize their chances at electoral victory. The problem with Cambridge Analytica's approach was that the firm engaged in psychological targeting using psychological data that was taken from millions of Facebook users, in most cases without the expressed knowledge or consent of said users. In addition to personality data gathered from online surveys, Cambridge Analytica's data mining activities also extended to the consumer realm, including brand and product preferences as well. Cambridge Analytica may have influenced the outcome of countless elections before the company's demise (and re-launch as Emerdata), but it did so unethically and at great cost to democratic processes around the globe. Cambridge Analytica violated user agreements by collecting large swaths of data that the company was not permitted to collect, and engaged in psychographic segmentation which then grew in stature to include data mining, predictive analytics and prescriptive analytics. Ultimately the company's actions were exposed, but not before purportedly influencing the outcomes of elections throughout the world.

Our fingerprints are all over, leaving clues about who we are and what we feel deep down. This demographic and, more importantly, psychographic information which was once considered property of the private unconscious domain now leaves digital clues with every click and tap. These clues turn into data, which in turn become inputs for algorithms that are programmed to appeal to our urges directly. What is imprecise today becomes increasingly precise with every new page, every new cookie. Our online behavior, then, can be thought of as a feedback loop in which our every action reinforces the system, making it more powerful with each successive interaction. Perhaps the next time you are scrolling through Youtube or Spotify and you see a gentle nudge, a simple suggestion, or a rudimentary recommendation, think about what that says about you, your lifestyle, and your preferences. After all, according to Michal Kosinski, if a software program or app is free, "then you are the product."[26]

This concludes our discussion of data analytics, which focused on the application of descriptive analytics, predictive analytics, and prescriptive analytics in both marketing and politics. In the next section, we will shift gears and examine how data analytics is used by marketers, and how it provides firms with untold creative potential value.

MARKETING ICEBERG

Chapter 5: Giving New Meaning to Old Traditions

Data on its own is meaningless, unless of course your business model is based on selling other people's data. Put differently, for the large majority of businesses, data is only valuable if it can be mined effectively. As we know, data mining gives purpose to structured and unstructured data by injecting them with meaning. As patterns and trends become evident, marketers are ideally positioned to take advantage of the insights they have gained from the data mining process. This chapter focuses on how marketers use data insights to create messaging and advertising that directly appeal to our emotions and sensibilities.

Much of the previous chapter focused on how our online behaviour can provide clues about who we are and what we are thinking. This is considered the analytical dimension of marketing. Marketers who engage in data mining effectively are not only able to predict the likelihood of future outcomes, but are also able to select from the most desirable future options in order to increase profitability. This chapter explores one central question: how do marketers take these potential outcomes and desirable options, and turn them into profitable returns?

If you remember back to our earlier chapters, you might recall us discussing how traditional marketing efforts have failed to give marketers the insights or results they desire, because they do not really delve into the unconscious domain. That is not to say that traditional marketing efforts, like billboards and other advertisements, are in themselves ineffective; rather, it is more about what purpose they serve and how best they can be used. These traditional marketing efforts can be combined with other tools to penetrate the minds of target consumers, and in the process influence their behaviour.

Imagine for a second you are required to cook two meals. The first meal is a simple breakfast for you and a friend to start your day. The second meal is a family feast full of tasty appetizers, mouth-watering entrees, and exquisite desserts. While you may be able to use some of the same tools to prepare both meals, like your trusty pan and spatula, it is likely you will need much more cookware, kitchenware, tools, and appliances to prepare the family feast than you will for the simple breakfast. Both meals involve cooking, plating and serving, but these processes will differ in degree and scope depending on the meal that is being cooked. Now, let us imagine there are two companies. One company provides a small selection of speciality consumer goods, while the other company provides a wide-variety of consumer goods at different price points which are suitable for people of all ages. The data you seek to mine will necessarily be different because the types of goods, the target market segmentation, and ultimately the appeal of the products differ greatly. Both companies engage in data mining, need tools to create prescriptive options, and require advertising to spread the word about their products, but these processes will differ in degree and scope depending on the type of company and goods. Successful companies engage in activities that are context-specific, meaning that the tools and messaging that they select are based on the unique circumstances of their target market and product.

Context is King

We should not overstate the importance of tailored, specific, actionable insights. Why? If your analysis is specific, then your advertising can be more precisely targeted, which allows your target market to respond more favourably to your advertising, which increases the likelihood of your returns being profitable. Traditional advertising, therefore, is far from useless. Messaging does impact our behaviour, just as brand identity impacts how we see ourselves engaging with a company and its products or services. Messaging and branding should not be your exclusive strategy, nor should it be an afterthought; instead, they should be the culmination of your data mining activities and epitomize the insights you have gained throughout the process. Consider the prior analytical activities as inputs into your eventual creative process. Without this, your creative activities will at best appeal to your market by chance, and at worse be completely off-base since it is not informed by any meaningful data.

Let us say you run a hygiene company that wants to sell diapers to parents. Perhaps you have different types of diapers, with each product line catered to a slightly different segment and offering its own unique benefits. Rather than choosing messaging and packaging colours based on your own preferences or what you think parents might like, you would be wise to first look at the data. How and to what extent do the target segments of each diaper differ? Which parent is likely to be shopping for diapers? What considerations play into that parent's mind when deciding on a particular diaper? What is the target parent's price sensitivity? Is the consumer eco-conscious? Is there a particular diaper line that is more suited to a specific age range? Data mining should provide insights into all of these areas and more, which better allows you and your marketing partners to choose colours, taglines, calls to action, and imagery that specifically caters to each segment of each product.

When we consider adding any new product or

service to our catalogues, we must subject this possible addition to rigorous data mining activities since the results of our analytical assessments will become the starting line of the creative process. We are taking an informed approach to our creativity when we pair our insights with colour theory, targeted messaging, effective calls-to-action, and seamless user experience. We are injecting our creative process with the same sort of purpose as our data mining activities, with one important difference: in data mining, we are trying to understand the impulses; in creative advertising, we are trying to use the impulses to influence behavior. It would be unwise to try to influence behaviour without knowing the impulses, and it would be a wasted business opportunity to know the impulses but not try to influence behaviour. Both are essential to the goal or purpose, which is to ultimately get your target to behave the way you want them to behave — whether that is buying a product, signing up to a mailing list, getting a donation to a worthy cause, or voting for a particular political party or candidate.

Remember Freud's iceberg from an earlier section?

When we move from data mining to creative advertising, we are moving steadily upward from our iceberg's under-water portion to its tip. Initially submerged deep below the surface, we find ourselves moving up the iceberg by understanding — through data mining and machine learning — details about our target market's unconscious feelings. When we have chosen our colour, messages, and other creative elements based on our target market's unconscious feelings, we are slowly turning these unconscious feelings into conscious opportunities to act. We find ourselves at the tip of the pyramid when our target market is behaving in a manner consistent with their emotions and thoughts, and consistent with the firm's goals. This is what I call analytic creativity, which in today's digital landscape confers limitless possibilities by bridging two previously distinct worlds — analytic and creative — into one.

Analytic Creativity

Analytic creativity is now the standard. Gone are the days when marketing was the exclusive domain of artists-turned-professionals. Any hope for a return to '60s- and '70s-era of advertising ended with Mad

Men's season finale. Today's digital Don Drapers are as creative as they are analytical. In order to produce great and impactful creative directions that move target consumers from thought to action, companies first equip themselves with tools to engage in data mining. The painstaking data mining work provides the insights necessary to start the creative process. Every creative decision from that point is guided by the data mining insights. When the analytical and creative dimensions are aligned, they together form a calibrated marketing strategy that is at once informed and effective. This unity is the goal of digital firms, who move seamlessly between the unconscious and conscious, devising new and interesting ways to uncover the unknown and use it for their own goals.

This chapter has focused on how digital firms use data mining insights to develop their creative, which in turn is used to appeal to our unconscious, changing our emotions and thoughts into conscious actions. Conclusions about the data become the starting point for creative activities, including messaging and colour schemes, which ensures that firms are engaging with their targets in a way that is aligned, calibrated and effective. We have spent a great deal of time, both in this chapter and in this book, on the unconscious mind and the opportunities which have presented themselves in light of big data in the digital era. It would be unwise to solely discuss the opportunities without discussing some of big data's troubling implications, namely the ethical, security and privacy concerns stemming from our online behaviour. In doing so, we may be able to better understand where we are, and how best to move forward.

MARKETING ICEBERG

Chapter 6: Ethics and Privacy in the Age of Big Data

The steady rise of big data has radically changed traditionally-run industries and even created new industries altogether, including artificial intelligence research, machine learning and advanced analytics. We will discuss in this chapter the implications of big data's steady rise, with particular attention paid to the ethical conflicts involving information access and data harvesting. We will also touch on the debate between security versus privacy, and how the very notion of privacy continues to change before our eyes.

In our chapter concerning psychographics, we discussed Cambridge Analytica and its ethically dubious, and otherwise illegal, activities related to its election activities. Part of the difficulty today is that we assume, anytime we "Agree" on an app's privacy policy, that firms are operating legally. Privacy policies in themselves are written in complex legal jargon and can exceed the length of even your most detailed encyclopedia, which makes it difficult to parse, let alone understand. We, as consumers, would likely be mortified to learn the true extent for which our data is being used. Companies simply require your agreement to use and even sell your information to third-parties, but how about those activities to which we have not given our consent? This is where firms like Cambridge Analytica get into trouble, because their appetite for data is so huge that they cannot satiate their hunger through strictly legal means. This is also where zero day vulnerabilities and backend permissions can create privacy nightmares for apps, much like the case was for Facebook. In fact, Cambridge Analytica breached Facebook's terms of service policies by acquiring through a third-party app the data on 87 million users — without their consent. Lawsuits and investigations abound, however can we ever get restitution or repayment for the improper use of our innermost details, especially when it concerns something as significant as influencing democratic election outcomes?

This seems to be at least part of the dilemma with this age of big data: Big data has enabled us to understand more about humans and behaviour than ever before, but it has also exposed us to the dangers of granting permissions to apps and services wholesale, without considering how they might be using them to influence our actions.

Advanced analytics, or business analytics, goes beyond just marketing. Take a second and think about all the different things you do with your phone. You use it to make calls, text friends, email colleagues, navigate to your destination, and peruse social media. Maybe you have notes on it about an upcoming project, or you paired your credit card to it to make purchases more seamless. All of this aggregated data is called metadata, which gives firms intimate details about who you are and what you have been doing. The metadata provides all the details, and while it may be accurate it is not necessarily the whole truth. Regardless, this information is used by marketers and consumer goods companies, but also intelligence contractors and "software" companies who promise security while helping to destroy hard-earned civil liberties at home and abroad.

Consider this: in the last ten years, we have been exposed to governments illegally collecting data, business firms misusing personal data, and software companies using innocent people's data against them. If we cannot trust governments, businesses, and software programmers to abide by strong ethical codes, then what hope is there for any shred of privacy to exist? Has society merely outgrown privacy, just as it outgrew typewriters and the Walkman?

Suffice it to say that our welcome embrace of, or acquiescence to, big data has utterly destroyed the traditional notions of privacy. What was once considered the private domain is now public; to the very least, it has exposed private details to people and machines beyond just ourselves and our devices. The opportunities in this space are significant, but so too are the consequences.

Creative Destruction

We have used the human mind and human behaviour to devise new and novel ways to solve problems, predict outcomes, and take advantage of opportunities. This has transformed sports, commerce, industry, and government. It has also led to data misuse and abuse, with private interests dictating the terms of service to people worldwide. This chapter is not meant to start a revolution, nor should it be viewed as an attempt to absolve firms and institutions from the responsibility to protect whatever remnants of privacy remain. Instead, we should strive to understand big data, business analytics, machine learning and the like as double-edged swords that create opportunities but also lead to consequences. We are left to contemplate whether these opportunities and consequences end up being positive or negative.

The scale of change has been rapid, and society has continued along by further immersing itself in a process of creative destruction. It seems society is constantly destroying the old as it creates the new. This persistent battle within creates tension between the old and new, and forces us to grapple with potentially uncomfortable ideas about who we are and our place within a complex ecosystem. This conflict is necessary because it compels us to make vital choices about the society we want to create. Except this time, we choose not just with our votes, but with every tap, click, and purchase.

That concludes our discussion about the implications of the unconscious, namely how personal data about our emotions and thoughts can be used for purposes that are beyond what we know, often for disturbing and troublesome reasons. These examples unfortunately are not isolated incidents, but by-products of big data. As we move further into the 21st Century, big data is poised to play a larger and more consequential role in our lives. As we equip ourselves with the knowledge and tools to better understand the world, we also have to understand that each one of us plays a vital role in how our world changes. The passive observer no longer exists.

MARKETING ICEBERG

Conclusion

This handbook explored how data scientists, using data mining and data harvesting, penetrate our minds, and in the process gain deep insights into our psychological behaviour. The unconscious mind has long perplexed researchers. Even dating back as recently as the early-20th Century, the unconscious mind was a great source of frustration for prevailing academic psychologists.

Freud likened the human mind to an iceberg which had three levels: the tip, the middle, and the submerged portions. The tip represents the conscious mind, which includes all of the accessible mental processes, like our thoughts and feelings. The iceberg's middle level consists of our preconscious, which are thoughts that may not be present in our mind but we can recall easily into our consciousness for use. Finally, we have the underwater portion of the iceberg called the unconscious, which is far greater in size than both the tip (conscious) and the middle (preconscious). The unconscious state can be considered a repository that has stored inside of it all of our repressed memories, feelings, thoughts, and the like. While Freud's theory of the unconscious may have lacked the same sort of scientific rigor as traditional psychological and scientific disciplines, his contribution was still significant. Freud was not the first to discern differences between our conscious state and our unconscious state, but he was instrumental in popularizing the distinction in the mainstream, which meant that the unconscious began to get the attention it rightfully deserved.

The unconscious went from being material that was great for cocktail parties, to becoming the guiding subject matter of academic research and studies. Dr. Gerald Zaltman, Harvard Business School Professor, knows this all too well, as the turn of the 21st Century brought with it new opportunities to understand human impulses. Zaltman has questioned the presumption that people actually know what they think. In doing so, Zaltman and other researchers have been instrumental in marketing's monumental change. Zaltman and Freud to the very least have shared a belief that humans are not necessarily truthful or forthright about certain thoughts and feelings, because these thoughts and feelings are driven by unconscious urges, like emotions, of which humans are unaware. Such urges are buried in the unconscious, and otherwise inaccessible to us. When called upon, we may respond with our beliefs, explanations and justifications, but these are just surface-level judgements; our true motivations lie somewhere beneath. It is difficult for us to say truthfully what we think when we do not know what we feel. Marketers had been placing too much stock in the 5 percent that was conscious, and had become misguided in their use of traditional methods to penetrate the 95% that was unseen. Interestingly, the conscious part of our mind goes to work almost immediately after the initial emotions have been registered in our body, by coming up with rational or logical explanations about those emotions. This can help justify the feelings in our minds, or even help us finally act on the impulses. In marketing, tools like surveys and focus groups may be useful depending on your predicament, your industry, your sector, and your ideal outcome; however, these tools are valuable only if they are catered to your situation, and you should consider all variables — including the drawbacks — prior to relying on these tools, and the data you get from them. When you are mindful and considerate of these dynamics, you can create interesting outcomes for your venture. The challenge for marketers was about taking these powerful symbols, and understanding them as a collection of actions.

HOW you segment your market matters. Psychographic segmentation involves categorizing or grouping potential consumers based on their personalities and individual characteristics. Psychographic segmentation, as the name alludes, refers to psychological traits — like personality attributes, values and attitudes, lifestyles choices, motivations, and priorities — that influence people's buying habits. Psychographic segmentation is not immediately data-centric because it is highly subjective, and hence it requires painstaking research and data collection in order to uncover the details. Despite the time and effort involved, there is considerable upside to the psychographic segmentation approach, namely that it allows marketers to understand their market's intricacies by cutting across demographic and geographic differences, and arriving at a more contextualized market segment.

Artificial intelligence strives to make simple the tasks that are complicated and tedious. In the span of a single day, we use artificial intelligence to unlock our phones (facial recognition), navigate our way to and from a destination (map software), decide on a purchase (search and recommendation algorithms), and even converse online with a company representative (receiving tech support online from a chatbot). Big data refers to the analysis of large amounts of data through non-traditional software. More specifically, big data can also refer to the methods used to extract value from data. Data can be structured or unstructured, which means that data can be organized and searchable, or data can be raw and free of a defined format. Data mining, a popular term in our digital world, refers to the practice of finding patterns in data. These data patterns are then used to identify interesting consumer and markets trends, which are subsequently used by businesses for targeting activities. No matter the objective, opportunities in the artificial intelligence space are plentiful. These opportunities arise when firms are able to capture large amounts of data, engage in data mining, and ultimately operationalize that data in ways where it targets specific emotions, eliciting the desired response from the target market.

Advanced analytics generally refers to a form of data analysis that uses sophisticated tools and methods to uncover insights and develop recommendations. These analytical tools and methods are considered advanced because they are able to conduct the complex types of analyses that traditional business intelligence cannot. Advanced analytics, or as it is sometimes referred to as business analytics, consists of three main subsets: descriptive analytics, predictive analytics, and prescriptive analytics.

Descriptive analytics is the most common of the three, and involves mining historical data to understand the reasons for past performances. Predictive analytics, like the name suggests, is focused on predicting likely future outcomes before they happen. Predictive analytics gives meaning to historical data by using algorithms, rules and possibly external data to identify trends and the probability of future outcomes coming to fruition. Predictive analytics is really about "what is likely to happen". Not to be outdone, prescriptive analytics is the third variety of advanced analytics. It does the job of predictive analytics, but also delves deeper into why certain events occurred; in doing so, prescriptive analytics provides myriad options about what to do and what not to do, as well as each option's implications. Prescriptive analytics, then, is not just about "what is likely to happen," but also about "what happens after that" and "what can we do to take advantage of what will happen". In this way, advanced analytics — through descriptive analytics, predictive analytics, and prescriptive analytics — can provide insights into the past, present and future, thereby improving a firm's likelihood of success.

Michal Kosinski is a Stanford University professor who holds a doctorate in psychology. Dr. Kosinski believes algorithms are full of potential, enabling pattern recognition and improving our predictive power. More specifically, algorithms are great at predicting human traits, like predicting specific emotions with a high degree of accuracy. Every time we do anything digitally, especially over the internet, we leave behind our digital footprints, which Kosinski contests amounts to 2 gigabytes per person, per day!

Firms engage in data mining to extract secondary data from this initial source. This can include more than just simple geographic location; in fact, if phone and software manufacturers know where you are, they can aggregate that data and extract even more information, including your lifestyle, religious and political views, health status, age, gender, and more. Equipped with this information, firms can target us with increasingly specific messaging that appeals directly to our urges, interests, values and preferences, all of which they know thanks to big data. We can see this in action every time we log into Youtube, Amazon, Spotify or Facebook. Any recommendations and suggestions are based on your digital footprint and are generated through data mining. Data analysts then use this data in algorithms that ensure any and all recommendations are in tune with your preferences.

Our fingerprints are all over, leaving clues about who we are and what we feel deep down. This demographic and, more importantly, psychographic information which was once considered property of the private unconscious domain now leaves digital clues with every click and tap. These clues turn into data, which in turn become inputs for algorithms that are programmed to appeal to our urges directly.

We should not overstate the importance of tailored, specific, actionable insights. If your analysis is specific, then your advertising can be more precisely targeted, which allows your target market to respond more favourably to your advertising, which increases the likelihood of your returns being profitable. Messaging does impact our behaviour, just as brand identity impacts how we see ourselves engaging with a company and its products or services. Messaging and branding should not be your exclusive strategy, nor should it be an afterthought; instead, they should be the culmination of your data mining activities and epitomize the insights you have gained throughout the process. Consider the prior analytical activities as inputs into your eventual creative process. When we have chosen our colour, messages, and other creative elements based on our target market's unconscious feelings, we are slowly turning these unconscious feelings into conscious opportunities to act. We find ourselves at the tip of the pyramid when our target market is behaving in a manner consistent with their emotions and thoughts, and consistent with the firm's goals.

Analytic creativity is now the standard. Gone are the days when marketing was the exclusive domain of artists-turned-professionals. In order to produce great and impactful creative directions that move target consumers from thought to action, companies first equip themselves with tools to engage in data mining. The painstaking data mining work provides the insights necessary to start the creative process. Every creative decision from that point is guided by the data mining insights. When the analytical and creative dimensions are aligned, they together form a calibrated marketing strategy that is at once informed and effective.

The steady rise of big data has radically changed traditionally-run industries and even created new industries altogether, including artificial intelligence research, machine learning and advanced analytics. Part of the difficulty today, though, is that we assume, anytime we "Agree" on an app's privacy policy, that firms are operating legally. Companies simply require your agreement to use and even sell your information to third-parties, but how about those activities to which we have not given our consent? This is where firms like Cambridge Analytica get into trouble, because their appetite for data is so huge that they cannot satiate their hunger through strictly legal means. This is also where zero day vulnerabilities and backend permissions can create privacy nightmares for apps, much like the case was for Facebook. Big data has enabled us to understand more about humans and behaviour than ever before, but it has also exposed us to the dangers of granting permissions to apps and services wholesale, without considering how they might be using them to influence our actions.

Suffice it to say that our welcome embrace of, or acquiescence to, big data has utterly destroyed the traditional notions of privacy. What was once considered the private domain is now public; to the very least, it has exposed private details to people and machines beyond just ourselves and our devices. The opportunities in this space are significant, but so too are the consequences.

We have used the human mind and human behaviour to devise new and novel ways to solve problems, predict outcomes, and take advantage of opportunities. This has transformed sports, commerce, industry, and government. It has also led to data misuse and abuse, with private interests dictating the terms of service to people worldwide. The scale of change has been rapid, and society has continued along by further immersing itself in a process of creative destruction. It seems society is constantly destroying the old as it creates the new. This persistent battle within creates tension between the old and new, and forces us to grapple with potentially uncomfortable ideas about who we are and our place within a complex ecosystem. This conflict is necessary because it compels us to make vital choices about the society we want to create. Except this time, we choose not just with our votes, but with every tap, click, and purchase.

While our time together has been brief, I hope this

book has provided you with some important insights that you can use to progress in your field of interest. Whether you are in business, politics, or any other area, it is vital that you have a strong understanding of the forces influencing your perception every day. I also hope this book has helped cultivate your interest in the new age of marketing, and given you a valuable foundation from which to grow.

MARKETING ICEBERG

ABOUT THE AUTHOR

FARHAD MORADI KOUCHI, an expert in the field of online marketing and web presence has been conducting consultancy sessions for different businesses in the past 15 years to help them better plan, setup, and manage digital communication strategies.

---

[1] Gilmore, H. (2017, July 4). ABC's of behavior antecedent-behavior-consequence. *Psych Central*. Retrieved from https://pro.psychcentral.com/child-therapist/2017/07/abcs-of-behavior-antecedent-behavior-consequence/

[2] Cherry, K. (2019, September 28. The preconscious, conscious, and unconscious minds. *Verywell Mind*. Retrieved from https://www.verywellmind.com/the-conscious-and-unconscious-mind-2795946

[3] McLeod, S. (2015). Freud and the unconscious mind. *Simply Psychology*. Retrieved from https://www.simplypsychology.org/unconscious-mind.html

[4] Ibid.
[5] Ibid.

[6] Ibid.
[7] Tulving, E. (1972). Episodic and semantic memory. *Organization of Memory*. New York: Academic Press

[8] Stroop, J.R. (1935). Studies of interference in serial verbal reactions. *Journal of Experimental Psychology*, *18*(6).

[9] Greenwald, A.G., and Banaji, M.R. (1995). Implicit social cognition: attitudes, self-esteem, and stereotypes. *Psychological Review, 102*(1).

[10] McLeod, S. (2015). Freud and the unconscious mind. *Simply*

Psychology. Retrieved from
https://www.simplypsychology.org/unconscious-mind.html

[11] Ibid.
[12] Bargh, J.A., and Morsella, E. (2008). The unconscious mind. *Perspectives on Psychological Science, 3*(1): 73-79. Retrieved from
https://www.ncbi.nlm.nih.gov/pmc/articles/PMC2440575/

[13] Ibid.
[14] Morse, G. (2002, June). Hidden minds. *Harvard Business Review*. Retrieved from https://hbr.org/2002/06/hidden-minds

[15] Ibid.

[16] Ibid.
[17] Ibid.
[18] Ibid.
[19] Yesbeck, J. (n.d). 4 types of market segmentation with examples. *Alexa*. Retrieved from
https://blog.alexa.com/types-of-market-segmentation/

[20] Ibid.
[21] DeCouto, C. (2020, April 27). Understanding Structured and Unstructured Data. *Sisense*. Retrieved from
https://www.sisense.com/blog/understanding-structured-and-unstructured-data/

[22] Interview with Michal Kosinski, "You are the product!," *Academia Superior*, April 15, 2019. Retrieved from

https://www.youtube.com/watch?v=uGjofTSMIHg

[23] Ibid.
[24] Ibid.
[25] Ibid.
[26] Ibid.

MARKETING ICEBERG

www.ingramcontent.com/pod-product-compliance
Lightning Source LLC
Chambersburg PA
CBHW070455220526
45466CB00004B/1831